THE BRAVE GIRL'S GUIDE TO WORK THAT YOU LOVE

Ashlene,

May you always do work that you love.

To your brilliance!

Tracy

THE BRAVE GIRL'S GUIDE TO WORK THAT YOU LOVE

TRACY IMM

ISBN: 1530363853
ISBN 13: 9781530363858
Library of Congress Control Number: 2016904134
CreateSpace Independent Publishing Platform
North Charleston, South Carolina

TABLE OF CONTENTS

Introduction

DIVINE DOWNLOADS ARE REAL

Dear Brave Girl,

Welcome and thank you for deciding to read "The Brave Girl's Guide to Work That You Love." My intention is to share with you a few tips and tricks that will help transform your work experience in this lifetime. Investing in your personal growth is SO important and my hope is to help get you motivated to find work that fills your soul. Your dream career is just around the corner. Know that I believe in YOU.

I knew that this book needed to be birthed when I had a "divine download" as I drove home from a speaking engagement at Towson University, a local college. I realized that my "little motivational speech" could potentially impact more women if I wrote it down into a book format. I had spent years learning lessons and I was getting results that others marveled at. One of my dearest friends calls me Super Woman and always ends our conversations with "You really do have a golden lasso." She makes me smile with that compliment.

You see to me, it was just who I was, how I was wired, what I was supposed to do --- so what's the big deal? Concepts that just seemed so simple to me were either not common knowledge, not well understood or just plain complicated to others. People did not connect the same dots that I did. What I came to realize is that it wasn't simple and straightforward to everyone else and I needed to use my superpowers for good. Hence, get writing. Write it all. Pour out my heart and soul. Share my gifts. Do it now or go home.

So I made a decision that I need to make myself visible and share. Be a BRAVE GIRL I told myself. It started with a vision to speak from the stage. To tell my story, share the lessons that I learned so that a younger version of me would not have to face the same struggles and issues. In other words, I decided to tell everyone what I would have told my younger self if I knew then what I know now.

Specifically I developed a signature talk for my undergraduate communications students who dreamed of a rock star career in public relations or corporate marketing. I called my talk "11 Ways to Rock Your Communications Career." I delivered it at industry conferences and to student groups and I got positive feedback every time I did it. I also got the haters who blasted me as I stepped out and became more visible. It took me a while to realize that their feedback had more to do with them and less to do with me but it still hurt. I kept speaking up. I continued to make myself VISIBLE as I shared my story.

I felt like I had done it all as a corporate executive and leader. I wanted to shed light for others. My students were eager, ambitious and hungry. My corporate world experience and advice was GOLD to them. The other professors were focused on sharing theories, not work war stories like I did.

My parents were teachers. They were supportive but did not have a clue about Corporate America and what it takes to thrive or survive. I felt lost and without a trusted guide. Not something I want for my worst enemy. You need mentors and guides. You need people who will have your back. I want to be that guide for YOU.

So my professional story and accomplishments went like this: I'd been a Director or Vice President for multiple Fortune 500 companies. I had stock options. I had seven figure expense accounts to hire multiple advertising agencies. I worked in eleven distinct industries. I hired and fired public relations agencies and employees based on their performance and contribution to the bottom line. I had done significant international business travel (complete with a driver) rubbing elbows with four-star generals at private parties at the US embassy. I organized corporate activity at international aerospace and defense trade shows. I hung out with Pentagon reporters and military top brass on a regular basis to talk military budgets, upcoming programs and invasions in Afghanistan. It was wild.

I'd organized Presidential tours of nuclear power plants. I had the opportunity to lead press conferences at the National Press Club in Washington, D.C. to unveil major billion dollar joint ventures in the nuclear energy industry. Afterwards, we'd schmooze on Capitol Hill and with the White House. I had done consulting to CEOs in multiple industries. I'd craft a comprehensive communications strategy and be asked to solve other complicated business issues for them. They knew me at private airports that NetJets served as I traveled with my C-suite clients on private corporate jets.

Never mind the employee communications campaigns that impacted 140,000 employees around the globe or the massive three-day corporate leadership events that transformed national and international organizations and helped them meet or beat earnings. I worked to establish and build investor relations functions for firms looking to go public. These were all run-of-the-mill projects and strategic initiatives that were just my life in the corporate world.

I tell you all of this information not to brag but to help you understand where I am coming from and what my corporate world looked like. However I confess to you - something was missing. I realized it was time to "Lean In" as Sheryl Sandberg said. Even more importantly, it was my obligation to give back as part of my legacy.

You see, I'd been in the shoes of my students and I wanted to shortcut their path to the top. I wanted to shout from the mountain top "don't do that", "make sure you do this" and "OMG, this is how it really is." The net result was a 45-minute inspirational and motivational talk that people loved and found helpful. My audiences told me that it was just what they needed to hear. It was perfect timing. It changed their thinking and sent them in another direction that made more sense. I was shocked, dazed and amazed at the impact. So I decided to keep offering it for free.

After I delivered my talk to 40 undergraduates nearing graduation in April 2014, I realized there were probably hundreds (if not thousands) who needed the same talk. When I planned my talk, I thought that it would be helpful to a core group of people.

DO YOU FALL INTO ANY OF THESE CAMPS?

* You are ready to transition to a new role or new employer
* You want to be doing what you were meant to do while on this planet
* You want to create your own path that leverages your gifts

So this e-book may be helpful if you find yourself in one of these three categories. Or it just might be the motivational pick me up that you were looking for. Better yet, it might be the right book to give to your niece or nephew or children as they leave the cozy world of academia and venture out into the "real" world. Whatever the reason, I am glad you are here and hope that this book adds a little value to your world, makes you think a little differently and just might lead to something great in your life.

As the great Eleanor Roosevelt said, *"you must do the things you think you can not do."*

In the end, I wanted to leverage the power of the Internet to impact more people, and not just communications students. In many ways, this is a self-help book that I wrote to myself and now I want to share it with you. I wanted to respect my divine download and make this real. So here we go!

Let your brilliance shine,

Tracy

Chapter 1

• • •

HOW TO HAVE AN AMAZING CAREER

One of my primary objectives in life (especially early on in my professional life) was to have an amazing career. I wasn't exactly sure what that would look like or how to achieve it but I knew I had to have it. I am the type of person who figures out what they want and then I go for it. It is part of my DNA. So starting in my senior year of college, I went to the races to figure out how to make it happen.

HERE'S WHAT I DID:

* I read books. Lots of them in fact. My favorite books are about leadership, business, marketing and technology.
* I talked to more senior and experienced professionals. I asked them to share their wisdom with me. Some of the questions that I asked them were:
    * How did they get to where they were?
    * What did they say was the reason they got the job they got?
    * What was their advice for me?

SOME OF THE OTHER ACTION STEPS I TOOK INCLUDED:

* I went to workshops, conferences, and seminars (often on my own dime).
* I volunteered at non-profits to get experience in areas that my employer would never let me experiment in. Thanks to the Junior League I was able to get experience in public policy. This led to corporate work in the world of legislative affairs. I was able to parlay several non-profit volunteer experience into paying gigs as a freelancer.
* I spent more money chasing the American dream than my tiny little budget could afford. I tried to find role models wherever I went.
    * I tried to work with people I admired.
    * I asked to be on exciting projects.
    * I asked for more responsibility.
    * I worked until 9 or 10 o'clock every night and came back at 7 in the morning to work some more. [Note: I don't recommend this one. It leads to burnout and frustration, not to mention strained relationships.]

But in the end, I got frustrated that *there was no silver bullet*. No simple solution. No straight path. No magic pill.

That said, I was determined not to go down without trying every angle. Many years into my career, I have learned that there is no set path. You need to just follow your heart. You need to listen to your intuition and if something does not feel right, then it probably isn't right. Learning the lesson that you are supposed to learn in that moment is important but we all have our own unique path to greatness that we will talk about later.

All in all, I have been very blessed to work for some great organizations that provided me with opportunities to excel. I've also learned some of the most painful lessons when I worked for some "not so great" bosses and just plain horrible companies. As new options presented themselves in the workplace,

I always wanted to be WILLING to accept the duties. I also wanted to be ABLE to take on the new challenge. This was really key in many cases to my promotions and big wins. Not to be all unicorns and rainbows, but I also worked really hard and never took anything for granted. Life is not always going to be fair, as much as you want it to be.

In my professional life, I've also gotten really clear about my values. I have an exercise that I walk my students thorough to help them contemplate and examine their top 5 values. [We'll cover this in Chapter 4]. What I have found is that when something does not feel right, there is usually a values conflict going on. Trust me on this one.

Now I have to warn you, that I have not completely mastered this topic of having an amazing career. In fact, I would tell you that it has been a hard and painful lesson for me to learn that rising to the top is not all that it is cracked up to be. You see, I have suffered major corporate burnout in my time. So much so that I had to take a medical leave of absence for six months to make sure I did not just collapse and drop dead. Yup, eight weeks on total bed rest with a strict restriction on all my activities followed by four months of no work or contact with work. No connectivity or connection to anyone at work. It was one of the saddest and most painful times of my life. Being the "Big Kahuna" as my dad says may not be all that you think it is.

Takeaway: Read Napoleon Hill's work, especially "Think and Grow Rich."

"Decide what you want, decide what you are willing to exchange for it. Establish your priorities and go to work."

– H.L. HUNT

Get your free bonus workbook at tracyimm.com/bravebonus

Chapter 2

● ● ●

CREATE YOUR PERSONAL ROADMAP

Every one of us has a unique path that we are on in life. It's up to each of us to create our own roadmap and not rely on someone else to take care of us.

The best advice I can give is:

* Start with yourself.
* Start where you are.
* Figure out your end game.

So here's what I mean:

Start with yourself. Many people don't have the personal fortitude to do the inner work that is needed to rise to the occasion. Dealing with your ego, your inner critic and other monsters under the bed is not easy work to do. My coach calls them Drunk Monkeys that you need to quiet. I love that. You need to not listen to them. It's much easier to blame, deflect and not accept total responsibility and ownership. However, when you accept 100% accountability for yourself, shifts occur. Count on it. Spend some time going deep. Spend money on therapy. Find a coach. Talk to mentors. The rewards are unbelievable. It starts with YOU.

Start where you are. It is what it is. Don't beat yourself up about where you are. Just get going from that place. So what if you have no experience. If you really want something, you will figure out a way to get that experience. Don't worry if someone else is starting at another place. It does not matter. Comparison is the thief of joy my friend. What matters is that you know where you are starting. This is **Point A**.

Figure out your end game. **This is Point B**. Think about a sports team and how they approach a game. The players and coaches know what they want to do (win, right?) and then they determine how to make it happen. Your life and your career are no different. Do you want to climb the corporate ladder to the highest level? Do you want to balance your work life so you can be a working mom with flexible work hours? Do you want to work only 20 hours a week? Only YOU know what your end game is. And it may shift over your working career and that is okay. I always liked to know where I was going to be in two years but that was just my personal preference. Knowing where Point B is helps guide your actions from Point A.

Only you can create your roadmap. Figure out Point B and then go about doing what you need to do to get there from Point A. I've done this exercise over and over again in my working life and it's served me well and I want that for you.

Know what you are looking for and make decisions accordingly. It's much easier to take action when you know what your Point B is. Your decisions should be easier to make. You can decide if you need to move, take a pay cut, accept a lateral position, take a new job or leave an organization when you take the long view. While it may not always be clear what your next step should be, it does help to map out the types of experiences you need to get or have in order to move towards your Point B.

WHAT DO YOU REALLY WANT?

Shift your mindset from playing small to playing big. Remember: **You are the CEO of your life**. You have to get your brain wrapped around this concept, even if you are still in college or in between jobs.

My challenge to you: Ask yourself "What legacy do you wish to leave?" One of the exercises you can do is to think about your funeral and obituary.

* What do you want people to say about you on that day?
* Did you make them laugh? Did you teach someone how to give back to the community?
* Were you a great spiritual being?
* What was your contribution to the world? It won't be about how many hours you worked or what company you worked for.

Make your choices accordingly.

Takeaway:

1. Create a life plan – I like what Michael Hyatt created but there are other ones out there. Here's the link to Michael's information: http://michaelhyatt.com/creating-your-life-plan
2. Another good resource is Tony Robbins. Read his blog on planning: http://training.tonyrobbins.com/meet-your-goals-with-massive-action-planning/#more-3127

"If you don't design your own life plan, chances are you'll fall into someone else's plan. And guess what they have planned for you? Not much."

JIM ROHN

Get your free bonus workbook at tracyimm.com/bravebonus

Chapter 3

● ● ●

GO DEEP AND DISCOVER YOUR WHY

What are you really meant to do while on Planet Earth? Think about your soul's purpose. The assignment you said yes to.

Now this is where it gets a little heady. We are talking DEEP. You really need to spend some time reflecting on this question. You also need to ask yourself what your big WHY is.

When you understand your life purpose and what you are really meant to do, it's easy to make decisions and take action. This is where people get all tripped up and waste a lot of time. I know I did. It seemed too esoteric to me and I preferred to push it under the rug and not deal with it. But when you spend the time to get real with yourself, you can sort through things a lot quicker. Having this clarity is important as you move through your working life. It can also help you decide if a particular organization is the right fit for you. Understanding more about yourself makes it easier to sell yourself to others who have the power to hire you, promote you and get to know you.

One of my favorite quotes is: <u>The Power of Purpose</u> by Ralph Marston

"Where there is purpose, there is energy. Actions directed towards a compelling purpose will create a powerful momentum that lines up events and circumstances in your favor. Purpose gives you a reason to get going each day and strengthens your determination to persist when the going gets tough. Purpose pushes you firmly towards your highest level of accomplishment."

What I have found to be true is that you should **"Do work that embodies who you are."** For example, if you thrive as a writer or graphic designer, then find work in that area. When you are in the zone it makes work not seem like work. If you find your unique strengths, then you can bring them to the table in a work setting.

Now go find your purpose and the energy will follow!

Takeaway: Watch Simon Sinek's Why TEDTalk and learn about the Golden Circle. Here's the link*:*
http://www.youtube.com/watch?v=sioZd3AxmnE

Get your free bonus workbook at tracyimm.com/bravebonus

Chapter 4

● ● ●

YOUR VALUES MATTER

I cannot stress enough how important it is for you to **know yourself and your values**. In this area, it is very personal to you AND it can change over time. There are several tools (free and for a fee) that can be used to help you in this area.

I've also worked with several executive coaches and organizational development professionals over the years to better understand my preferences and style versus my peers and colleagues. When I understood preferences and styles, it helped me figure out how to talk to people the way that they preferred. My results improved when I better understood these concepts. Some of the tools that I have worked with include Myers-Briggs, DISC, and Kolbe Strengthfinder to name a few.

Take time to review your core values on a regular basis. This can be as simple as listing the top five values that are most important to you.

GAINING CLARITY ON YOUR VALUES:

Circle ten values that resonate with you. Now select the top five that are non-negotiable. My coach first introduced me to this exercise and I now share it with my students. This is a hard exercise for many people because we don't give a lot of thought to it. Trust me, this is a really important review to do on a regular basis because when your work is not in alignment with your values, conflict arises. Remember that. If you find yourself unsatisfied or discontent with your work situation, ask yourself if the work environment is in alignment with those top 5 values you have selected.

Here is a list of values for you to get you started:

Accomplishment
Accuracy
Adventure
Affection
Balance
Bravery
Celebrity
Challenge
Comfort
Commitment
Control
Courage
Dependability
Directness
Efficiency
Enthusiasm
Expertise
Fairness
Faith
Flexibility
Generosity
Health
Honesty
Impact
Independence

Intelligence
Justice
Kindness
Leadership
Learning
Love
Mindfulness
Peace
Power
Punctuality
Reliability
Respect
Security
Sincerity
Spirituality
Spontaneity
Strength
Success
Teamwork
Understanding
Vision
Wealth
Winning

*"When your values are clear to you,
making decisions becomes easier."*

Roy E. Disney

Takeaway: Buy Tom Rath's book, "Strengthfinders 2.0" and take the survey.

Chapter 5

● ● ●

LEAD, EXECUTE, INFLUENCE

If you have any desire to rise in corporate America or within your profession, then you have to be a LEADER. Individuals who can lead people, projects and organizations are usually the most highly compensated. Learn everything you can about leadership by studying others, reading books and getting advice from leaders that you respect. If you can execute and implement projects successfully (meaning: on time and under budget) you will be rewarded and recognized. An even more important characteristic is the ability to INFLUENCE. We'll tackle that concept later in the chapter.

Innovate and be an early adopter. Another way to stand out is to innovate. If you are forward thinking and can see what's around the corner for your organization, then you can bring solutions to the table when most people don't even see the problem yet. When you are an early adopter, you can add value in many ways. Often times, the top of the company is looking for new revenue opportunities and you may be able to make a recommendation that they have not thought of or considered.

Demonstrate bold enthusiasm. Strong leaders often are the best cheerleaders, whether it be for their people or a particular initiative. Their enthusiasm can be contagious. You can stand out with your higher ups when you create positive momentum for your work group or your activities.

Be generous and care about people. The best leaders also tend to be generous with their time, talents and financial resources. The leaders that I have the utmost respect for genuinely care about people and they are not afraid to demonstrate it. When you are generous, people pick up on that energy. When you respect and care about people it shows and others pick up on that energy too.

Connect with people and bring them UP. Even if you are not an extrovert, it's important to connect with people and bring them up (no matter how down you might feel). This is especially important when you are in a leadership position (or have aspirations to be in a leadership position). While we all have down days (or weeks, months or years), it's your attitude that can be a deal breaker. You'll stand out if you can make personal connections and get people motivated to take on a particular task or project. Plus it's just more fun to work with positive people, right?

People "buy" from you when they know, like and trust you. Some people call this the KLT factor. If you think about your own buying experiences, then you can probably agree with this concept. I know I am much more likely to do business with people that I know, like and trust. It's just makes the whole experience that much more enjoyable. It's why things like Angie's List came into being. The same is true in the corporate space where teams are buying your ideas and talents.

Take 100% responsibility. Know that you have to work on **yourself** first to improve any situation. Shifting or placing blame on others is completely non-productive. Again, taking 100% responsibility is the way to go.

"The quality of a leader is reflected in the standards they set for themselves."

RAY KROC

Takeaway:

*   Study principles of Leadership.
*   Read John Maxwell's books.
*   Follow Brendan Burchard.

Get your free bonus workbook at tracyimm.com/bravebonus

Take My Quiz: *How Influential Are You Within Your Organization?*

WHEN EXECUTIVES OF YOUR COMPANY MEET, DO YOU HAVE A SEAT AT THE TABLE?

a) EVERY TIME! (Give yourself 10 points)
b) Sometimes (Give yourself 5 points)
c) I did not even know there WAS a meeting (Work to be done, my friend – 0 points)

HOW MUCH DOES YOUR OPINION HOLD WITHIN THE ORGANIZATION?

a) We consistently implement my ideas and solutions (Give yourself 10 points)
b) Every once in a while management listens to what I have to say (5 points)
c) No one listens to me, including my direct supervisor (0 points)

HOW OFTEN DO YOU HAVE FACE TIME WITH SENIOR LEADERSHIP?

a) I routinely meet with senior leadership (10 points)
b) I have spent time with senior leadership but it's rare (5 points)
c) They have no clue who I am (0 points)

ARE YOU KNOWN BY COLLEAGUES AS A STRATEGIST OR A TECHNICIAN?

a) I am routinely thought of as a strategist (10 points)
b) It's a mixed bag; some people see me as a strategist while others see me as a technician (5 points)
c) Most everyone views me as a tactical implementer (0 points)

HOW OFTEN IS YOUR OPINION SOUGHT OUT FOR HIGH-LEVEL PLANNING?

a) I am usually the one driving the bus when we meet and I propose the strategy (10 points)
b) Every once in a while senior leaders ask my opinion or include me in the high-level planning meetings (5 points)
c) What's high-level planning? (0 points)

DO YOU FIND MOST OF YOUR TIME IS SPENT PUTTING OUT FIRES?

a) Yes, I am the best fire fighter in the department (Sorry you get 0 points)
b) Some of my time is spent putting out fires (5 points)
c) No, I have solid processes and systems in place so there are not many fires (Congrats you get 10 points)

DO YOU HAVE A CLEAR VISION ON HOW YOU WOULD LIKE TO BE PERCEIVED BY COLLEAGUES? IS IT WORKING?

a) Yes, I am perceived as a strategist by most if not all of my colleagues (10 points)
b) Some people perceive me as a tactician while others see me as a strategic business partner (5 points)
c) No, I really don't and I have no idea how I am perceived (0 points)

HOW MUCH TIME DO YOU SPEND STAYING CURRENT ON THE LATEST TRENDS, TOOLS AND STRATEGIES?

a) I am strategic and I invest a lot of time learning what's hot and what works for organizations like mine (10 points)

b) Occasionally I will surf the web to see what's happening (5 points)

c) I have a degree…What more do I need? (0 points)

HOW MUCH TIME DO YOU SPEND THINKING ABOUT WAYS TO ADD VALUE TO YOUR COMPANY AND ITS STAKEHOLDERS?

a) It's all I really focus on (10 points)

b) Every once in a while I give it some thought (5 points)

c) I've never given it a moment of my time (0 points)

HOW CRITICAL IS THE ROLE THAT YOU PLAY WITHIN YOUR ORGANIZATION?

a) My role is a critical leadership role for our organization (10 points)

b) I support many activities but I could be replaced tomorrow (5 points)

c) The company could decide to eliminate my position tomorrow and no one would notice if the position were filled or not (0 points)

SCORING:

* *0-50 points mean: It's critical that you develop a plan ASAP*
* *50-80 points mean: Your plan needs work to get you a seat at the table on a consistent basis*
* *80-100 points mean: Congratulations on being a person of influence and having a seat at the table!*

Chapter 6

● ● ●

NEVER STOP LEARNING

Both of my parents were teachers and I have loved school my whole life. I remember "playing school" with my younger sister in our basement growing up. I really believe that we should never stop learning. I especially emphasize this with my undergraduates when they think they are "done." **You're never done**. Some of the most successful people invest time and money on their personal growth and development until the day they die.

We've all heard stories of 90 year olds getting college degrees or 50 year olds changing professions after obtaining degrees. I have a friend who trained as a teacher and taught in New York City schools. But in her mid-30s, she decided that she really wanted to be a doctor. So she quit her job, took out student loans and went to med school and guess what? She's a doctor now. Living her dream and impacting people in amazing ways. She's also teaching and training other doctors. She goes on mission trips to Ethiopia and donates her time and talents to underserved Africans who can't afford healthcare and she finds it immensely fulfilling. Now this is someone who understands that you never stop learning.

The fact of the matter is **you'll never know it all. You can always learn from others.** I always try to learn from others that I work with. Age doesn't matter. I learn from more experienced workers. I learn from Millennials on my teams. I learn from my customers. I learn from my suppliers and vendors. Being a giant sponge every day makes for a fulfilling work and personal life. If I learn a new word or concept, I write it down and teach it to one other person. Think of everyone as your teacher and your student.

Assimilate your learning from experiences, books, seminars. I admit that I am a learning junkie. I read books. I find seminars to attend. I find free webinars to listen to. I listen to podcasts in my car. But what I find most beneficial is turning all of these information sources into tangible things I can integrate into my life. It's a waste of money to participate in these types of activities if you can't implement them in your day-to day activities.

Ask yourself "what can I learn from this?" When you experience a rough patch or problem there is always a lesson to be learned. If you keep experiencing the same problem over and over again that just means you have not yet learned the lesson.

Who inspires you? What can you learn from this person? There are so many people that inspire me and I regularly tell them when they have inspired me. Find reasons to inspire others, too.

Takeaway: John Maxwell, a Christian leadership expert, recommends that before you go to bed each night you ask yourself these questions:

* What did I learn today?
* What spoke to both my heart and my head?
* How did I grow today?
* What touched me and affected my actions?
* What will I do differently? Unless you can state specifically, you haven't learned anything.

"There is no end to education. It is not that you read a book, pass an examination, and finish with education. The whole of life, from the moment you are born to the moment you die, is a process of learning."

JIDDU KRISHNAMURTI

Get your free bonus workbook at tracyimm.com/bravebonus

Chapter 7

● ● ●

COMMIT TO ONE HOUR OF STUDY DAILY

*"One hour per day of study will put you at the top of
your field within three years. Within five years, you
will be a national authority. In seven years, you can be
one of the best people in the world at what you do."*

EARL NIGHTINGALE

Attaining expert status in your field takes time, dedication and commitment. When you are "all in" people see that. They gravitate to you. When you love a particular topic, you can easily immerse yourself for an hour a day. You get in the zone and you thirst for that new knowledge. It does not seem like work.

Early on in my career, I found it fascinating and interesting to study leadership, technology, business, project management, marketing and communications. I sought out seminars, books and experiences that would teach me as much as possible about these topics. I looked for work opportunities that would put me at the nexus of these topic areas. I worked for large organizations that had communications needs with many stakeholders. They also needed massive enterprise systems to run day-to-day operations and I always wanted to work with company leaders. I came to understand how these systems get evaluated, procured, budgeted for, implemented and maintained.

I also tried to find projects that were led by strong business leaders. I wanted to support these projects and the leaders that ran them with strategic communications and change management outreach to end users. It became easy to find an hour a day to learn about leadership, business, project management, technology, marketing and communications. You can do the same. Pick your field, pick your interests and then go find ways to learn more. Watch what happens.

If you are in transition or just starting in your field, you may have to get creative. You may have to find internships or volunteer opportunities with little to no pay to get you started. For example, there are tons of non-profits that have needs you could help fulfill such as grant writing, event planning, fundraising, marketing and administrative tasks that support other functional areas like finance and operations. If you are passionate about a cause, then start there. Build those relationships with key staff and ask what needs to be done. You can develop a reputation as a reliable resource that they would be happy to recommend or provide a reference for.

The other recommendation that I have is to take the long view when you undertake your daily hour of study. As you take these baby steps, one day you will wake up and be a subject matter expert. The level of effort you put in will show up down the road. Keep at it. Luck happens when PREPARATION meets *OPPORTUNITY*. You want to be prepared.

Takeaway: Study and read about trends, benchmark best practices, undertake new experiences.

Chapter 8

● ● ●

PROTECT YOUR BRAND. BE A MOVIE STAR IN YOUR OWN LIFE. ATTRACT YOUR AUDIENCE.

In today's 24/7/365 connected world, it's more important than ever to protect your brand. It's all you've got really. So be intentional. Be thoughtful. Be purposeful as you shape it. Show up the right way. You need to be both interesting AND remarkable.

In teaching undergraduates, I like to share with them that employers WILL check your social media posts when you apply for a job and they will monitor them while you work there. This should not be a shock to them but it is. As you define your dreams, you'll want to be positioned to share your gifts with the world.

So let's talk a little about your brand. Just like the big consumer brands like Volvo, Wal-Mart and Coca-Cola, we each have our own personal brand to consider. Study what these brands do to shape their image. Determine the attributes you want people to use to describe you and your body of work.

My desire is for my personal brand to be described as: SMART, CONNECTOR and AUTHENTIC.

I feel like they best describe who I am and how I want to be perceived by others. I want to use my brains, personality and self to make the world a better place and I want to share my gifts in this way. An example of this is writing this book to help people like you!

There is only one YOU. What three words describe your personal brand? Write them here:

1. _____
2. _____
3. _____

KNOW WHAT IT TAKES TO STAND OUT.

I recommend to my students that they follow personal brand experts to better understand this concept. Read books in this area to get ideas on ways to brand yourself. Learn how celebrities come to be known by just their first name. Think Oprah, Cher, Madonna and Ellen. Their personal brands attract a certain audience and you can too. If there is someone in your field or industry that appeals to you, note what they are doing to brand themselves. It does not have to be shameless self-promotion. It's about being authentic.

TAKEAWAY:

Follow and engage with personal branding experts like these gurus:

1. Robin Fischer Roffer of Big Fish Marketing: http://bigfishmarketing.com
2. William Arruda, The Personal Branding Guy: http://www.williamarruda.com
3. Jennifer Ransaw-Smith of BrandId, a Brand Elevation firm: http://www.brandidsp.com
4. Amanda Miller Littlejohn: http://www.amandamillerlittlejohn.com

"You have to think of your brand as a kind of myth. A myth is a compelling story that is archetypal, if you know the teachings of Carl Jung. It has to have emotional content and all the themes of a great story: mystery, magic, adventure, intrigue, conflicts, contradiction, paradox."

DEEPAK CHOPRA

Get your free bonus workbook at tracyimm.com/bravebonus

Chapter 9

● ● ●

SHIP IT

Ever wonder how some people just get promoted, and promoted and promoted while you sit by and stay in the same job? I know I did. Well the fact of the matter is they get stuff done. That's the magic formula.

Seth Godin called this "how much have you shipped" phenomenon. When I first heard this theory, I didn't quite get it. I have to be honest with you. I was that clueless. However, once I started practicing it amazing things started to happen in my work life. Basically, he says figure out what needs to get DONE <u>today</u> and do it. I put a Post-It note on my computer monitor that said "Did you ship it?" to remind myself.

It's been interesting to keep track of what I've shipped and how quickly I've been given additional responsibilities and garnered the respect of people who matter. Don't just come to work to collect a paycheck and take up air. You don't want to be that person. You'll go nowhere fast and potentially even be walked out the door. When times get tough, businesses will keep the valuable contributors before the deadbeats.

I recommend that you practice shipping things every day for a month and the results will be amazing. I've also implemented it in my personal life and it's moved me along on things I have procrastinated on for years. Dragged my feet. Never taken action. Even doing the next logical thing. They are now done or on the path to being done.

At the same time as you are busy shipping things every day, you need to be appropriately engaged with what is going on and deciding what NOT to be engaged in. Half the battle may be to leave some things undone at the end of the day. Today may not be the best day to take action. Evaluate in the morning whether you need to tackle that particular task. Trust me on this one.

If you need help with time management or productivity, then go to training, read a book or find a mentor who you think is good at getting things done. One person that I find helpful is David Allen who specializes in helping people be more productive.

The bottom line: Solve the most pressing and interesting business problems for the organization. Get relevant things done. Let the urgent but not important stuff GO. Track your progress.

Takeaway:

1. Read David Allen's books on Productivity. His website is: http://gettingthingsdone.com
2. Read Seth Godin's books. His website is: http://www.sethgodin.com/sg/

> *"It's okay. Let your ego push you to be the initiator. But tell your ego that the best way to get something shipped is to let other people take the credit. The real win for you (and your ego) is seeing something get shipped, not in getting the credit when it does."*
>
> SETH GODIN

Chapter 10

● ● ●

CONQUER YOUR FEARS

If you've never read "A Course in Miracles", put it on your list of books to read. In that book, Marianne Williamson said, *"Our deepest fear is not that we are inadequate. Our deepest fear is that we are powerful beyond measure. It is our light, not our darkness, that most frightens us."*

Everything is possible but you need to conquer your fears. They say that FEAR stands for False Evidence Appearing Real. This is absolutely what's going on. Until you confront what's holding you back, you'll stay right where you are. Some of the common fears we have include: fear of poverty, fear of failure, fear of public speaking, fear of flying, fear of heights. When you detach from the outcome, you can often overcome your fear. When you take that next logical step, you can overcome your fear. Push your limits.

I like this quote from David Neagle that says *"We fear what other people will think of us. You may need to change who you spend time with. What are you afraid you will lose if you are a terrific success?"*

When you get serious about tackling your fears, shifts will occur. Denial is not a good long-term strategy if you want to be successful. Dig deep on why you have a particular fear. Most of the time, the root cause of your fear does not even make any sense. Ask yourself why you are allowing this fear to hold you back. If you need outside help from a therapist or counselor, get it.

Takeaway: Listen to David Neagle's The Art of Success Business School (free) podcast on iTunes.

"Everything you want is on the other side of fear."

JACK CANFIELD

Get your free bonus workbook at tracyimm.com/bravebonus

Chapter 11

PRACTICE PATIENCE

One of the hardest lessons for me to learn has been to practice patience. My grandmother used to tell me in her sweet little church lady voice, "Now Tracy, Rome was not built in a day," when I would whine to her about my frustrations. You see God has a plan for all of us and it will happen in his time, not ours.

When I started to be truly grateful for everything I had, the miracles started to flow. Forcing things to happen only made matters worse. Letting go and trusting the Universe is so liberating. It's hard to do. It takes practice. It takes persistence. When you don't understand why certain things are happening, know that there is always more going on than you can see.

Helen Keller said, "When one door of happiness closes, another opens, but often we look so long at the closed door that we do not see the one which has opened for us." This is true and I've experienced it multiple times in my professional life. I bank on it now.

If you don't already subscribe to Mike Dooley's daily Notes from the Universe emails, sign up here: http://www.tut.com/inspiration/nftu.

I got this Note from the Universe one morning and I posted it on my corkboard at work to remind me to practice patience. It worked. I calmed down. Here's what it said:

It's perfectly normal, Tracy, that when waiting for a really big dream to come true it seems like it's taking forever, you wonder if you're doing something wrong, and you feel like you should just be happy with less.

But I promise you, no matter how long it takes, once it happens it'll seem like time flew, you'll wonder how you ever doubted yourself, and you'll feel like you should have aimed a little higher.

Aim a little higher, Tracy.
The Universe

TAKEAWAY:

*   Learn how to meditate.
*   Do yoga.
*   Just breathe.
*   Follow Gabrielle Bernstein @spiritjunkie.

> *"Patience is not simply the ability to wait - it's how we behave while we're waiting."*
>
> JOYCE MEYER

Get your free bonus workbook at tracyimm.com/bravebonus

Chapter 12

DEVELOP THE MINDSET OF A WINNER

A positive attitude can make all the difference in the world. You see it in sports, theater, and politics. The person who believes she can, does. Having a winning mindset can propel you across the finish line, land a plum assignment or win office.

One of the easiest ways to develop the mindset of a winner is to be with positive people. Jim Rohn said, "You are the sum of the five people you spend the most time with." When I heard this, I listed those five people to figure out if they were the five I should be spending my time with and honestly, I dropped one --- my boss at the time.

Yup, he wasn't good for me. I spent tons of time with him. Yet, he brought me down. Destroyed my confidence. Marginalized me. Vetoed every idea I had. Made me feel bad, unworthy, stupid, crazy. That's when I realized it might be time to move on. So I took the risk to find a new job where I was appreciated, celebrated, rewarded, recognized for my contributions and able to implement my ideas. And the Universe responded. I feel like a winner now. So thank you Jim Rohn for sharing your little observation. It made a difference.

Dennis Waitley said, "*The reason most people never reach their goals is that they don't define them, or ever seriously consider them as believable or achievable. Winners can tell you where they are going, what they plan to do along the way, and who will be sharing the adventure with them.*"

I think he's right. You do need to define your goal and believe they are achievable. You should be able to tell people where you are going and what you plan to do along the way and who will be with you.

The field of positive psychology is interesting to learn and can help you develop that winning mindset that you'll need. There are many motivational speakers and experts that can help you in this are. Think Tony Robbins, Shawn Achor, Martin Seligman, Barbara Frederickson.

Many times, you are SO close to achieving your goals that you may want to give up. Don't do it. Keep the faith; stay positive and think like a winner.

Takeaway: Read Barbara Frederickson's work on positive psychology: http://www.positivityratio.com/index.php

"Many of life's failures are people who did not realize how close they were to success when they gave up."

THOMAS EDISON

Chapter 13

FEEL CONFIDENT. BE CONFIDENT. IT MATTERS.

A lack of confidence protects you from moving forward and possibly growing. People can sense if you are not confident and some will attack you,
undermine you and just generally make your life miserable. Starting today,
commit to work on your confidence. People want to work with people who are
confident (not arrogant). Your self-esteem needs to be strong.

What I have learned is that you have to TRULY want to be confident.
Then you have to act as if you were that confident person until you don't have
to act anymore. When you believe in yourself and what you can accomplish,
you're unstoppable. Be confident in who you are and what you stand for so
you can truly inspire people to achieve extraordinary results. You really can
"Own the Room" as they say.

Think about a time when you encountered someone who lacked confidence. Then think about a person who exudes confidence and how that made
you feel. How do you want people to feel about their dealings with you? That's
right – you want them to do business with you.

On the flip side, when you come across as overly confident that can back-
fire and people may be turned off. It's a tricky balance that takes practice. You

need to be humble and approachable yet strong in your outward appearance and opinions. Ask your closest friends or your family to tell you how they perceive your confidence level. They will share the truth (even if it hurts!) and this gives you a baseline to work from. When you have set backs, often you will be more resilient the more confident you are.

Whatever has happened to you in the past needs to get resolved in order for you to have confidence. My advice is to do whatever it takes to work through those issues or it will hamper your ability to move forward and can potentially diminish your self-confidence.

TAKEAWAY:

* Read Rosabeth Moss Kanter's book called "Confidence"

"Believe in yourself! Have faith in your abilities!
Without a humble but reasonable confidence in your
own powers you cannot be successful or happy."

NORMAN VINCENT PEALE

Get your free bonus workbook at tracyimm.com/bravebonus

Chapter 14

HOW TO HAVE AN AMAZING LIFE

*First, have a definite, clear practical idea: a goal,
an objective. Second, have the necessary means to
achieve your ends: wisdom, money, materials, and
methods. Third, adjust all your means to that end.*

ARISTOTLE

It took a major crisis occurring with my health followed by losing my job three times (yes I said three) to realize that it was way more important to have AN AMAZING LIFE than being Super Woman at work. With an obsession to rise to the top, I had successfully comprised my personal relationships, my health and effectively lost my way. By being singularly focused on just one element of my life, I put myself at risk. And I had no clue.

With each sudden jolt that I felt each time my job got eliminated, I realized that it's not healthy to define yourself only by your job, no matter how big your paycheck or how fancy your title. I don't want this for you. You deserve more. You just do. And I hope this e-book helps you in some small way.

It was in my time of crisis that I found out who my true friends were. I came to appreciate the depth of love my family had for me. I saw that life is short. I also realized that I needed to express my gratitude for the blessings in my life that had NOTHING to do with my employer, my paycheck, my expense account, or my title. I tell you this because I don't want you to fall into the same trap as me. It's not a fun place to be. In fact, it totally SUCKED.

Whether you are just entering the work world or you are "in transition" (code for in between jobs), know that balancing time and money is an art, not a science. As you go through life, it's a constant battle that you need to master. Depending on the stage of life that you are in, you may find that you have lots of money and no time – good for the bank account, bad for relationships and allowing you down time to rest. The flip side is lots of time and no money. A total bummer if you like to shop, travel or enjoy the finer things in life.

So where do you start with creating an amazing life? Think mind, body and spirit. By taking care of yourself first in these three areas, you will be able to give more generously to others and not just to work. One way you can create an amazing life is to set goals in the area of family & friends, fitness, spirituality and hobbies.

Takeaway: Create a personal creed to guide your life.

Here is mine:

In planning my weeks and days, I focus on key roles and goals to maintain balance and perspective.

I am a responsible, kind, loving, trustworthy and supportive spouse. I give priority to this role. To keep this relationship healthy, I make daily deposits in the emotional bank account of Donald.

In my family of origin and extended, I want to build healthy, loving relationships in which we let each other become our best selves. I see my family as one of my greatest treasures. I will forget the mistakes of the past and press on to greater achievements in the future.

In all that I undertake, I will deal with others with sincerity, integrity, honesty, tolerance, compassion, evenness, and consideration. I acknowledge that exercising integrity is a moment by moment choice. I choose to work towards what I want to be, do and have.

I will live my life without excessive indulgences, aware that my mind and body are my true assets. I believe in God and am committed to a lifetime of prayers and meditation. In my daily endeavors, I avoid neither risk nor responsibility, nor do I fear failure, only lost opportunity.

Throughout my life, I choose to focus on the positive, to work within my circle of influence – to act directly on things I can do something about and thereby reduce my circle of concern.

In all areas of my life, I strive to be a Win-Win person, possessing integrity, maturity and an Abundance Mentality. I will work towards Win-Win relationships to establish high levels of trust. I practice the art of empathic listening in all areas of my life. Listening with my eyes, ears and heart helps me to understand feeling, meaning and context.

I commit to this Personal Creed today and plan to review it frequently to ensure that I am living it.

Frame your personal creed. Put it in a place where you'll see it.

Do regular check-ins with yourself on how you are doing. Be honest. Course correct if you need to but don't beat yourself up if you haven't made it to the gym six days a week or if you haven't prayed every day.

Baby steps. Baby steps.

You want to look back on your life and say "Now that was amazing."

You can do this. You SO can.

> *"Twenty years from now you will be more disappointed by the things that you didn't do than by the ones you did do. So throw off the bowlines. Sail away from the safe harbor. Catch the trade winds in your sails. Explore. Dream. Discover."*
>
> *ARISTOTLE*

Get your free bonus workbook at tracyimm.com/bravebonus

Conclusion

PULLING IT ALL TOGETHER

I hope by now you've uncovered a few pearls of wisdom or learned about someone you may not have heard of that will help you on your journey. Many of the concepts and ideas that we've covered are not new or novel but may be new to you. My wish is for you to take what makes sense for you and take the next logical step. I'm a firm believer that everything happens for a reason. You read this book for a reason. It's what you needed now to get you what you want in the future.

I organized this book to make it easy to read. That was on purpose. With the pace of life these days, we need to be able to take small bites but come back for more when we are ready. My hope is that you find a takeaway that can be easily implemented this week whether it's reading a book, finding a mentor or signing up for a seminar. You could even start to follow some of the thought leaders mentioned in the book.

I also challenge you to think more broadly and strategically. Step back and take the long view on your work and personal life. The two are intertwined and you'll be so much happier when you step into what you are supposed to during your time on Planet Earth.

It really is time for your brilliance to shine.

Wishing you much joy, happiness and peace now and forever!

Tracy

Get your free bonus workbook at tracyimm.com/bravebonus

AUTHOR BIO

With nearly three decades of experience in corporate America—often as a company's only female executive—Tracy Imm is passionate about conveying her knowledge of personal and business success to anyone seeking career advancement.

Based on her experience in twelve distinct industries, Imm's writing and public speaking events are geared toward inspiring people to achieve their dream careers.

Imm is an accredited business communicator, and she holds certifications from the International Association of Business Communicators and the Public Relations Society of America. Outside the boardroom, she has earned numerous awards for her community service work with nonprofits.

She currently lives in Baltimore, Maryland, with her husband.

RESOURCES

This book is filled with recommendations for successfully navigating the corporate waters and your personal life. If you are comfortable tackling the suggestions that I've made, then I suggest you get started. If you feel that you would benefit from a more structured approach to implementing many of the suggestions, here are some additional tools and resources to consider.

E-Newsletter: The Point
Sign up to receive my e-newsletter, The Point, where I share insights, tips, and more. You can sign up at tracyimm.com. I promise to never share or sell my list!

Influence Audit
This free downloadable online tool— found at tracyimm.com —walks you through a series of diagnostic questions that help you determine how influential you are in your current organization.

Free Brave Girl PDF Workbook
This free downloadable PDF workbook— found at tracyimm.com tracks the chapters in this book, offering a set of guided questions and prompts to help

you get the most out of the book, decide what changes to explore, and lay out a plan of action.

Online and On-Site Training

For a more hands-on or in-depth training experience tailored to you or to your organization's specific needs you may also want to explore our live and virtual trainings and consulting. You can find more information on these at tracyimm.com.

Speaking

To book Tracy Imm for a speaking engagement, you can find more information at tracyimm.com, or contact her via e-mail (booking@ tracyimm.com) or telephone (443.650.8674).